THE
STRESS
FREE
START-UP

Simple Steps
To Make Starting
A Profitable Business
Fast, Easy, & Fun

by
Rachel Wolfinbarger Jimenez

GENERAL DISCLAIMER

This publication and the accompanying materials are designed to provide accurate and authoritative information in regard to the subject matter covered in it. It is provided with the understanding that the publisher is not engaged in rendering legal, accounting, or other professional opinions. If legal advice or other expert assistance is required, the services of a competent professional should be sought.

The educational training program provided hereunder is not designed or intended to qualify students for employment. It is intended solely for the avocation, personal enrichment, and enjoyment of students.

FORMS DISCLAIMER

All forms contained herein are provided for educational purposes only. The provider does not assert any warranty, express or implied, as to the legal effect and/or completeness of the forms. The provider hereby disclaims any and all liability with respect to these forms. The provider suggests that you contact an attorney to ensure that the forms are modified to meet the laws of your state.

DISCLOSURE FOR THE STRESS-FREE START-UP

The Stress-Free Start-Up is intended to provide generalized broad-based experiential training. This information is not intended to provide legal advice or detailed guidance on how to properly conduct business in your state. As with any regulated activity, we strongly recommend that you consult with an attorney. There are a growing number of states that have enacted legislation that could impact how you participate in business activities in those states. Violations of these laws may result in civil and criminal penalties, including damages, fines and terms of imprisonment. For more information about these laws, please consult with an attorney.

Although the author and published have made every effort to ensure that the information in this book was correct at press time, the author and publisher do not assume and hereby disclaim any liability to any party for any loss, damage, or disruption caused by errors or omissions, whether such errors or omissions result from negligence, accident, or any other cause.

FIRST EDITION

Book design and layout: Andrew Hall | www.hallisticdesigns.com

ISBN 978-0-9963324-1-5

Are you ready to play the most exciting game of your life?! This workbook will take you through a self-paced and self-guided journey to help you conquer fear, hesitation, and perfectionism so that you can be empowered and launch a business that makes money now.

While you can go on this journey alone by going through the workbook, I highly recommend that you find other people who also want to start or grow a business, and make this journey a friendly competition (key word here: FRIENDLY). Having other people go on this journey as well will help you when you get stuck and hold you accountable to take action. The friendly competition will encourage you to focus on progress instead of perfection, and keep you moving forward.

If you choose to compete with other people, I would recommend that you all agree to help each other by holding each other accountable, brainstorming, and giving honest feedback. Also agree to not sabotage each other. This game is about everybody growing and building more confidence while making more money.

So, how do you get started? Read the information below to get started.

BEFORE YOU PLAY

- Find one to ten people who would like to be a part of the Stress-Free Start-Up (if you're having trouble finding people who want to start a game, try going to meet up groups, Facebook groups, or local SBA offices to find people who would be interested).
- Make sure each person has a copy of the Stress-Free Start-Up workbook.
- Find an impartial and trusted third party to act as the "point keeper". The point keeper will be responsible for tallying the scores every week, and posting them so everybody knows where everyone else stands. The point keeper is a great role for a teacher, chamber of commerce employee, business coach, or consultant.
- Decide if you want to "make the game interesting". To make it interesting, each player can give an agreed upon amount of money to the point keeper who will award the entire pot of money to the person who earns the most points at the end of the game.
- Decide if the players would like to meet on a regular basis to help each other and brainstorm how to move forward. If yes, decide how often, when, and where (weekly or bi-weekly meetings are helpful in holding people accountable).
- Determine the start and end date of the game (recommended time period: no longer than 90 days).

GAME OBJECTIVE

- Get out of your comfort zone and create a business that makes the most money within a set period of time (no longer than 90 days).

HOW TO PLAY

GETTING POINTS

- To hold you accountable to do the tasks required in the Stress-Free Start-Up workbook, each "challenge" will be awarded 10 points once completed.
- Because business requires you to get out of your comfort zone, players are awarded 20 points every time they get rejected (see glossary for specific definition of a rejection).
- Since the main goal is to monetize the business, 100 points will be awarded for every $1 that is sold and collected.

POINT KEEPER

- By being the point keeper you agree to being an impartial third party, to judging fairly and honestly, and to being the safe keeper of the funds if the group decides to "make the game interesting".
- Once the group has been formed, ask the group if they'd like to "make the game interesting". If yes, determine how much money each person will put into the pot. Set a date when the money will be due, and the game will start. If people do not turn in the money, they should not be allowed to compete.

HOW TO SCORE:

- Each "challenge" will be awarded 10 points once completed. (Ask to see the workbook, and make sure it has been completed, or have them take a picture and send it to you to prove they've done the exercises).
- Because business requires you to get out of your comfort zone, players are awarded 20 points every time they get rejected (see glossary for specific definition).
- Since the main goal is to monetize the business, 100 points will be awarded for every $1 that is sold and collected (ask for proof).
- A sell only counts if the money has been collected. Ask for proof.

KEY COMPONENTS OF A REJECTION:

- An offer that costs money was made to someone
- The player received a negative response (ex. "no", "not now", "I can't", "I can't afford it", "I'm not interested", etc.)

TRACKING THE POINTS:

- Tally the points as you go in an excel document so you can keep a running tally. It's helpful if the group sets up a private Facebook group where they can ask each other questions, post success stories, and also see the points so they know where everyone is in the competition.

CHOOSING A WINNER:

- The winner is the person with the most points at the end of the Stress-Free Start-Up. If you decide to "make the game interesting", the winner receives the entire pot.

- If the points are even, the person with the most sales wins.
- If the points and sales are even, there will be a tie breaker day, and the person who sales the most in that day will be the winner.

- Rather than posting the final scores, I recommend that everybody gets together for a final meeting and the point keeper announces the winner in a grand ceremony! It will make it more fun.

GLOSSARY

- Rejected: somebody communicated that they have decided not to buy your product or service after you've made them a specific offer and asked for the sell. The following count as rejections:
  - You talk to somebody (in person, over the phone, via personal email, Facebook messenger, or live chat) and eventually ask them if they would like to buy your product or service and they say no (in some way, shape, or form). No response does not count as a rejection.
  - You teach a class or workshop, and make a specific offer at the end. Everybody who attended the workshop for the first time that didn't buy counts as a rejection.
  - You teach an online webinar, and make a specific offer at the end. Everybody who stayed for the ENTIRE webinar that didn't buy counts as a rejection.
  - The following do NOT count as rejections:
    - You talk to people about your business, but never make them an offer.
    - You teach a class or workshop but never make an offer.
    - You send out a mass email with an offer in it to 100 people and no one buys your product or service.
    - You pass out 1000 flyers and no one buys your product or service.
    - You send someone a private message and offer something, but they never respond to you.

FAQs

- *Can people participate in the game as teams?*
  - Yes, as long as everyone in the game agrees that this is okay.
- *If we decide to "make the game interesting", when should people give their money to the point keeper?*
  - It's important that the point keeper receives the money before the start day of the game.
- *How can this game be done in less than 90 days?*
  - Follow the workbook, but do multiple challenges per day to make it go by more quickly. For example, if you'd like to finish the game in 30 days, complete 3 challenges a day (90/30=3).

• *If somebody is making money from many different products and/or services, do those count towards them receiving points for the game?*

- Yes, multiple products or services count. For example, if somebody decides to be a personal trainer and sell their services, but they also sell weight loss equipment - the money from both items will count towards their points. Furthermore, if somebody has multiple ideas and makes money from different products or services those all count towards their points.

TIPS AND TRICKS

• I highly recommend that you try to get your daily "challenge" completed by 10am each morning. This will relieve stress, and will give you a feeling of success. Try not to overthink anything, but rather, trust the process, and take action. If you need help, ask for it! (I can't stress this enough).

MY HOPE FOR YOU

"

And for this year, my wish for each of us is small and very simple.

And it's this, I hope that in this year to come, you make mistakes.

Because if you are making mistakes, then you are making new things, trying new things, learning, living, pushing yourself, changing yourself, changing your world. You're doing things you've never done before, and more importantly, you're doing something.

So that's my wish for you, and all of us, and my wish for myself. Make new mistakes. Make glorious, amazing mistakes. Make mistakes nobody's ever made before. Don't freeze, don't stop, don't worry that it isn't good enough, or it isn't perfect, whatever it is: art, or love, or work, or family, or life.

Whatever it is you're scared of doing, DO IT.

Make your mistakes, [this] year and forever.

"

- Neil Gaiman

To your glorious mistakes and the success that follows!

Much love,

Rachel Jimenez

Founder of TalkRaw.org

&

Creator of *The Stress-Free Start-Up*

WELCOME!

ACTION:

*the process of doing
something, especially
when dealing with a
problem or difficulty*

Thank you for investing in the Stress-Free Start-Up! I'm excited to take you on an exciting personal and professional journey that can provide you with real monetary results! Remember, this program is about action. I highly recommend you take action before moving on to the next challenge. Also, you will have more fun and get more done if you compete with a friend or group of people. Check out the Stress-Free Start-Up Game Rules for more information about how to play the game.

PROGRESS

The daily "challenges" will start off easy, but will progressively get more difficult. In the beginning, you will do a lot of self reflection exercises. These are vital in building the foundation to your business. Do not skip these. Trust the process. You will need the information gained from the reflective challenges as you progress through the game.

If you need help, motivation, inspiration, support, or guidance, lean on other people participating in this challenge and/or the other members of the Stress-Free Start-Up Facebook group.

KEYS TO SUCCESS

I highly recommend that you try to get your daily "challenge" completed by 10am each morning. This will relieve stress, and will give you a feeling of success. Try not to overthink anything, but rather, trust the process, and take action. If you need help, ask for it!

RESOURCES WHEN YOU'RE STUCK

• Post your need to the Stress-Free Start-Up Facebook Group

• Talk to other people participating in the Stress-Free Start-Up

• Ask a mentor for help

CHALLENGE 01

WHAT DOES THE WORLD SEE AS YOUR GIFTS?

Many times it can be difficult for us to know what our own strengths are. The old expression of "not being able to see the forest for the trees" rings true for most people. So, to welcome you to the Stress-Free Start-Up, and give you an easy task, today, all you have to do is ask 5 people that know you well the following questions:

- What they think you are good at
- What they admire about you
- What they see as your strengths

If you feel weird asking people these questions, here are some tips:

1.) I want you to feel weird! Business owners have to do things the average person doesn't normally do, so get comfortable feeling uncomfortable.

2.) Feel free to blame me and the Stress-Free Start-Up for this exercise – just start a call, conversation, text, email, or letter with something like

"One of my goals for this year was to start/grow my business, I signed up for a program to help me achieve that goal in 90 days, and the first action item is to ask 5 people these questions...Can you please do me a favor and reply with honest answers by the end of the day?"

3.) 100% of the people you contact may not respond to you. To increase your odds of getting responses back from 5 people you may want to reach out to more than 5 people.

Record the answers to each question in the following sections. Fill in the blanks at the top of the page with the name of the person you asked. READY? GO!

_____ says	_____ says	_____ says	_____ says	_____ says
I'M GOOD AT:	I'M GOOD AT:	I'M GOOD AT:	I'M GOOD AT:	I'M GOOD AT:

ADMIRES: ADMIRES: ADMIRES: ADMIRES: ADMIRES:

sees these	sees these	sees these	sees these	sees these
AS MY STRENGTHS:	AS MY STRENGTHS:	AS MY STRENGTHS:	AS MY STRENGTHS:	AS MY STRENGTHS:

ONE DAY DOWN! SEE THAT WASN'T SO BAD!

CHALLENGE 02

LIMITING BELIEF:

a belief that is not true and limits your ability to reach your full potential

CHALLENGE YOUR LIMITING BELIEFS

Many of our foundational beliefs are formed from early childhood experiences, and were established to help protect us in some way. However, as we grow, beliefs that were meant to serve and protect us at one time start to limit us and hold us back. These beliefs that hold us back are known as "limiting beliefs".

Here's a common example: When we're young, most of us heard "Don't talk to strangers" at one point or another. This message was meant to protect us from talking to people who could do us harm. For many children, however, their young brain internalizes a deeper message that "strangers are bad and/or scary." While this message protects young children, if they never challenge this original belief when they are adults they can feel nervous and insecure when they have to talk to strangers at a job interview, when they need to network to grow their business, or even if they simply need to ask for directions.

When a foundational belief causes you anxiety, it is limiting you and needs to be challenged and eliminated. Follow the steps below to confront and eliminate your limiting belief. See the end of this challenge for an example of my limiting belief and how I overcame it. If you have more than one limiting belief (I know I do), then you can repeat this process to eliminate those as well...

STEP 1: KNOW WHAT YOUR LIMITING BELIEF IS

What does the little voice in the back of your head tell you all the time that holds you back from reaching your full potential? Write the answer below.

MY LIMITING BELIEF IS:

....

....

....

....

Here are some possible examples of possible limiting beliefs:

- I'm too young

- I'm too old

- I don't have the energy

- I don't have the money

- I hate selling

- I don't like talking to people

- I'm not good/smart/pretty/talented/popular/etc. enough

If you know where your limiting belief came from, write down that story as well in the section below (see example on page 16 if necessary):

MY LIMITING BELIEF CAME FROM:

....

....

....

....

STEP 2: PROVE YOURSELF WRONG

Once you know what your limiting belief is and where it came from, you need to prove to yourself that it's no longer correct. To do this, you will need to find 3 examples from your own life that prove your limiting belief to be wrong. You should also find 3 examples from outside your life that prove your limiting belief wrong. Finally, ask supportive people in your life to give you 3 examples that prove your limiting belief to be wrong so you can make a strong case against your limiting belief.

3 EXAMPLES FROM MY OWN LIFE THAT PROVE MY LIMITING BELIEF WRONG:

1.) ....

2.) ....

3.) ....

3 EXAMPLES FROM OUTSIDE OF MY LIFE THAT PROVE MY LIMITING BELIEF WRONG:

1.) ....

2.) ....

3.) ....

1.) ....

2.) ....

3.) ....

BELIEF:

an idea one accepts as being true or real

STEP 3: REWRITE YOUR BELIEF

Simply knowing your belief is no longer true will not eliminate it. To truly eliminate your limiting belief, you need to replace your limiting belief with a liberating belief. Here's an example of a format you can use to rewrite your limiting belief.

I may be .... (objective fact) but I was/I am also .... I've .... (accomplishment) which has helped others .... (result you've provided).

If I don't share my (knowledge/skills/passions) with people, I'm doing the world a disservice.

STEP 4: REPEAT YOUR NEW BELIEF STATEMENT TO YOURSELF EVERY DAY

Going through this exercise once and expecting your limiting belief to be eliminated simply won't work, and here's why: your subconscious has repeated your limiting belief over and over again in your mind. To combat your limiting belief, you need to repeat your new belief to yourself every day to drown out the negative little voice in the back of your head. Trust me on this. Read your new belief to yourself first thing in the morning and before you go to bed at night. It's also helpful to read this statement to yourself when you feel like you're lacking confidence.

Remember, if you have another belief that's holding you back, feel free to repeat this process.

STEP 1: KNOW WHAT YOUR LIMITING BELIEF IS.

My limiting belief is:

"I'm too young (notice that young is subjective, not objective), nobody will listen to what I have to say."

My limiting belief came from:

I'm the "baby" in the family and when I was a small child I would want to do what my sister (who is 7 years older than me) was doing. People would tell me I couldn't do what she was doing because I was too young. Now I realize that they were just trying to protect me because it wouldn't make sense for a 7-year-old to go to a high school party, for example.

STEP 2: PROVE YOURSELF WRONG

3 EXAMPLES FROM MY OWN LIFE THAT PROVE MY LIMITING BELIEF WRONG:

1.) I have my MBA.

2.) I've taught and counseled hundreds of people and helped them start businesses when I worked at a women's business center.

3.) I've worked at multiple start-up companies and helped them start and grow their companies.

3 EXAMPLES FROM OUTSIDE OF MY LIFE THAT PROVE MY LIMITING BELIEF WRONG:

1.) Mark Zuckerberg started a business at 19, and was a billionaire by the age of 23.

2.) Bella Weems started Origami Owl when she was only 14 years old with only $350, and now it's a multi-million-dollar company.

3.) Mike Cachat, from Riverside, California (a city near my home town), started selling bike parts when he was only 16 years old, and now his business makes over 25 million dollars a year!

3 EXAMPLES FROM SUPPORTIVE PEOPLE THAT PROVE MY LIMITING BELIEF WRONG:

1.) Brittany said that I've inspired her to start her own business, and helped her make and save over $8,000 this year.

2.) Kasey told me she went from lacking complete confidence and wanting to give up to making over $1,300 in 90 days because of working with me.

3.) Mahum told me she got clarity and focus and with the actionable steps I provided and she learned how to take productive actions towards her goals while moving past her fears to make the money she wanted.

STEP 3: REWRITE YOUR BELIEFS

"I may be in my twenties, but I was born a naturally inquisitive leader. I've coached and trained hundreds of people from 16 to 60, and I've helped them quickly and efficiently develop ideas, create products, and take action, all of which has lead them to making thousands upon thousands of dollars. If I don't share my knowledge with people, I'm doing the world a disservice."

STEP 4: REPEAT YOUR NEW BELIEF STATEMENT TO YOURSELF EVERYDAY

I repeat my statement to myself in the morning when I wake up and in the evening before I go to bed. I also repeat the statement if I'm about to do something outside of my comfort zone.

I'd love to see the before and after of your beliefs. Please share them with the Stress-Free Start-Up community on Facebook.

MY NEW BELIEF IS:

CHALLENGE 03

WHY :

*for what reason
or purpose*

WHY ARE YOU DOING THIS?

Have you ever set a goal and had problems achieving it or felt afraid, uneasy, or like giving up? If you have, don't worry because you're not alone. Also, don't blame yourself; you simply didn't have the right tools to keep you motivated.

Today we're going to help you build some things to lean on when you start to feel like giving up because inevitability, over the next 90 days, you will encounter some challenges.

The first step is to think about your motives... take a few minutes to reflect and answer the following questions:

WHY DID YOU/DO YOU WANT TO START A BUSINESS?

....

....

....

....

WHAT PAIN WILL STARTING/GROWING A BUSINESS HELP YOU AVOID?

....

....

....

....

....

....

....

....

....

....

It helps if you dig deep, and try to connect to your own emotional triggers, stories, and examples from your own life. For example, one of the reasons I started the Stress-Free Start-Up is because my two-year-old puppy, a Yorkie-Chihuahua mix named Bella, got hit by a car and died. I was, and still am devastated by that experience, but it taught me that life is short, and we never know when we're going to be gone so we have to make our time here worthwhile. While that seems to be totally unrelated to business, if I'm feeling unmotivated, I think back to that life lesson that I had to learn the hard way, and I get moving on my goals.

Use this space to reflect on your own emotional triggers, and life lessons that can motivate you to get moving:

....

....

....

....

....

....

....

....

The next step is to identify what inspires you. I personally am inspired by up-beat music and hearing stories of other people doing amazing things with their lives so I constantly listen to empowering music, read autobiographies, and listen to podcasts that interview amazing people that have done amazing things. When I need a boost, I can lean on what inspires me to find motivation.

INSPIRE:

fill with the urge or ability to do something, especially something creative

SO, WHAT INSPIRES YOU? (BE SPECIFIC)

....

....

....

....

....

....

....

The final step is to set up positive and negative reinforcements for yourself related to your goals.

FIRST, START BY DETERMINING WHAT YOU WOULD LIKE TO RECEIVE AS GIFTS OR REWARDS (BE SPECIFIC AND GIVE A RANGE OF INEXPENSIVE AND EXPENSIVE GIFTS OR REWARDS YOU CAN GIVE YOURSELF):

....

....

....

....

Next, determine when you will be able to collect your reward. Since we haven't specifically discussed goals yet, we're just speaking in generalities here.

FOR EXAMPLE, TO STAY MOTIVATED, WILL YOU NEED TO GET REWARDED WHEN THE GOAL IS OFFICIALLY FINISHED, OR AT VARIOUS CHECKPOINTS ALONG THE WAY?

....

....

Finally, *give yourself a budget for your rewards*, and if you don't have a budget use this space to come up with rewards you could give yourself that are free (e.g. test driving a fancy car, going for a hike, or reading a great book).

....

....

....

ADDITIONAL THOUGHTS:

CHALLENGE 04

WHAT ARE YOUR GOALS?

Goals. They're important. In the book, "What They Don't Teach You in Harvard Business School", Mark McCormack mentions a fascinating study conducted on the 1979 Harvard MBA program where graduate students were asked "have you set clear, written goals for your future and made plans to accomplish them?" The results:

- 3% of students had written goals and plans
- 13% of students had goals, but they weren't in writing
- 84% of students had no goals at all

Ten years later, the same group was interviewed again and the result was absolutely mind-blowing. The 13% of the class who had goals, but did not write them down was earning twice the amount of the 84% who had no goals. The 3% who had written goals were earning, on average, ten times as much as the other 97% of the class combined! While this study only looks at earnings to quantify success, I still find it to be an extremely motivating example of why creating clear and measurable goals and writing them down is a key to success.

The first step to setting clear goals is to simply come up with a vision for your life and what you want. So, set a timer for 10 minutes, and then imagine the next piece of paper is magical and that whatever you write on it will come true within the designated time frame. Think of it as a wish list describing your ideal life. Think big. Take notes of details, and be specific. Try to think about what your day looks like in your ideal life: where you are living; what you see; who you are with; what you feel, smell, taste, and touch; and what you're accomplishing. Don't worry about being "realistic," just have fun. Ask yourself this question:

"If you could have anything, be anything, or do anything, what would it be?"

VISION

Now that you have a vision, go back and circle the one goal from each of the 4 sections that would have the MOST positive impact in your life.

The next step is to rewrite these four BIG Goals and then make them "SMART" which stands for specific, measurable, attainable, risky, and timely.

Start by simply rewriting your big goals below (don't worry about making them "SMART" just yet):

LIFETIME GOAL: ....

....

....

....

....

....

3 YEAR GOAL: ....

....

....

....

....

....

1 YEAR GOAL: ....

....

....

....

....

....

3 MONTH GOAL: ....

....

....

....

....

....

Now, you're going to rewrite your goal one more time, but this time make sure that it has the following characteristics:

SPECIFIC

Clearly defined and identified, helps you understand specifically when you've achieved your goal.

MEASURABLE

Able to be measured to help you understand your progress related to reaching your goal successfully.

ATTAINABLE

Something that you desire and are capable of achieving.

RISKY

Is a big enough stretch to push you outside of your comfort zone.

TIMELY

Will be completed by a specific due date.

Goal: Lose Weight

SMART Goal: I will lose 20 pounds by working out (specific) 3 times a week (measurable, attainable, and risky) and eating less (specific) than 1800 calories of real food every day (measurable, attainable, and risky). I will accomplish this goal by December 31 (timely).

SMART Lifetime Goal: ....

....

....

....

....

....

....

SMART 3 Year Goal: ....

....

....

....

....

....

....

SMART 1 Year Goal: ....

....

....

....

....

....

....

SMART 3 Month Goal: ....

....

....

....

....

....

....

Also, don't forget to use the information from yesterday to set a reward for achieving each of these goals (the bigger the goal, the bigger the reward):

Lifetime Goal Reward: ....

3 Year Goal Reward: ....

1 Year Goal Reward: ....

3 Month Goal Reward: ....

CHALLENGE 05

STOP MAKING EXCUSES

We all have the same amount of hours in a day. So how do Beyoncé and Mark Zuckerberg create empires? Easy! They prioritize, do what's essential, remember what motivates them, delegate, and they stop making excuses.

PRIORITIZE

When thinking of what to do with your time, ask yourself, "What task can I do right now that will get me closer to my BIG goal?" Then do that task, and leave the other ones for later.

DO WHAT'S ESSENTIAL FIRST AND FOREMOST

Continue to ask yourself, "Is this the highest and best use of my time?"

REMEMBER WHAT MOTIVATES YOU

Review your notes from challenge 3 when you're feeling unmotivated.

DELEGATE

If someone can do something better than you, or the task doesn't move you closer to achieving your big goal, delegate it.

STOP MAKING EXCUSES

Excuses are there to protect our ego, and let us feel good about ourselves even when we're not doing what we said we were going to do. Before you start making excuses, preemptively establish ways to overcome excuses to get the tasks done that will lead you to your goals. Here's how:

WHERE ARE YOU GOING TO FIND TIME AND MONEY TO START AND GROW THIS BUSINESS? WHAT DO YOU HAVE TO GIVE UP TO MAKE ROOM TO ACHIEVE YOUR GOALS? WRITE YOUR ANSWER IN THE SPACE BELOW:

....

....

....

Now, think about excuses you commonly use and ask yourself what you can do, and/or what you have to give up to overcome that excuse and achieve your goals. Repeat the previous questions for your main excuses and write the answers below:

EXCUSE	WHAT CAN I DO, AND/OR WHAT DO I HAVE TO GIVE UP TO OVERCOME THIS EXCUSE AND ACHIEVE MY GOALS?
I don't have time	I can wake up earlier and spend less time browsing Facebook or other social media sites.
....	....

CHALLENGE 06

COME UP WITH IDEAS BASED ON YOUR PASSIONS & STRENGTHS

If you're going to create a business and a life that you love, you may want to focus on your passions and strengths. Take a few minutes out of your day to reflect on the following questions and write down the answers. Feel free to borrow ideas from what your friends said on challenge one if they relate to your passions. If you're already in business, I would suggest you try to openly participate in this exercise, you might be surprised at the results.

WHAT DO YOU WISH YOU COULD DO ALL OF THE TIME?

....
....
....

WHY?

....
....
....

HOW DO YOU LIKE TO SPEND YOUR WEEKENDS?

....
....
....

WHY?

....
....
....

IF A LONG-LOST RICH UNCLE WROTE YOU A CHECK FOR $5 MILLION, HOW WOULD YOU SPEND YOUR TIME (AFTER ANY INITIAL TRAVEL AND SHOPPING SPREES WERE DONE)?

....

....

....

....

WHY?

....

....

....

....

WHAT WOULD YOU DO IF YOU KNEW IT WAS ABSOLUTELY IMPOSSIBLE TO FAIL?

....

....

....

....

WHY?

....

....

....

....

Now, compare your passions to each other and circle the top two areas of passion from above.

Next, write the two passions that you circled in the appropriate blank on the following page, and write down all of the steps associated with each of your passions in the STEPS column on the next page. As you look at each step ask yourself "what do I find annoying or frustrating about this step?" This will help you identify pain points associated with each step. Write down these pain points in the PAIN POINTS column on the next page (see example below as a guide).

AREA OF PASSION #1: DOGS

STEPS	PAIN POINTS
Walking Dogs	Pulling on Leash
Training Dogs	Finding the Time
Picking Up Dog Poo	Smelly, Gross, Time Consuming
Cleaning Up After Dogs	They can destroy furniture
Finding Dog Sitter	Expensive, Time Consuming
Taking Dog to Vet	They get nervous

AREA OF PASSION #1: ....

STEPS	PAIN POINTS

AREA OF PASSION #2: ....

STEPS	PAIN POINTS
....	....
....	....
....	....
....	....
....	....
....	....
....	....
....	....
....	....
....	....
....	....

Next, circle the top four most painful pain points and label them numbers 1 to 4, then ask yourself, how will this pain point be addressed 2 years from now? How will it be addressed 5 years from now? Write your answers below:

AREA OF PASSION #1: ....

SOLUTIONS TO 1ST PAIN POINT: ....

....

SOLUTIONS TO 2nd PAIN POINT: ....

....

SOLUTIONS TO 3rd PAIN POINT: ....

....

SOLUTIONS TO 4th PAIN POINT: ....

....

SOLUTIONS TO 1ST PAIN POINT: ....

....

SOLUTIONS TO 2nd PAIN POINT: ....

....

SOLUTIONS TO 3rd PAIN POINT: ....

....

SOLUTIONS TO 4th PAIN POINT: ....

....

Each of the pain points and solutions are actually potential customer needs and the foundation to a new business idea. Circle the top business idea.

Another great place to find inspiration for business ideas is by looking at your strengths. Take a few minutes out of your day to day to reflect on the following questions and write down the answers. Again, feel free to borrow ideas from what your friends said on challenge one if they relate to your strengths.

WHAT ARE YOU REALLY GOOD AT?

....

....

....

WHAT DO YOU DO BETTER THAN ANYONE YOU KNOW?

....

....

....

WHAT COMES EASILY TO YOU?

....

....

....

WHAT DOES YOUR DAILY ROUTINE CONSIST OF?

....

....

....

....

....

....

WHAT ARE YOU ASKED FOR HELP WITH MOST OFTEN?

....

....

....

*NOW, COMPARE YOUR STRENGTHS TO EACH OTHER AND CIRCLE THE TOP TWO
FAVORITE STRENGTHS FROM ABOVE.*

Next, write the two items that you circled in the appropriate blank on the following page, and write
down all of the steps associated with each activity in the STEPS column on the next page. As you look
at each step ask yourself "what do I or others find annoying or frustrating about this step?" This will help
you identify pain points associated with each step. Write down these pain points in the PAIN POINTS
column on the next page.

SKILL SET / STRENGTH #1: ....

STEPS	PAIN POINTS (FOR YOU OR OTHERS)

SKILL SET / STRENGTH #2: ....

STEPS	PAIN POINTS (FOR YOU OR OTHERS)

Next, circle the top four most painful pain points and label them numbers 1 to 4, then ask yourself, how will this pain point will be addressed 2 years from now? How will it be addressed 5 years from now? Write your answers below:

STRENGTH #1: ....

SOLUTIONS TO 1ST PAIN POINT: ....

....

SOLUTIONS TO 2nd PAIN POINT: ....

....

SOLUTIONS TO 3rd PAIN POINT: ....

....

SOLUTIONS TO 4th PAIN POINT: ....

....

STRENGTH #2: ....

SOLUTIONS TO 1ST PAIN POINT: ....

....

SOLUTIONS TO 2nd PAIN POINT: ....

....

SOLUTIONS TO 3rd PAIN POINT: ....

....

SOLUTIONS TO 4th PAIN POINT: ....

....

Each of the pain points and solutions are actually potential customer needs and the foundation to a new business idea. Circle the top business idea.

CHALLENGE 07

COME UP WITH IDEAS BASED ON YOUR EXPERIENCES

Another great place to find business ideas is based on your life's experiences. Your unique life experiences hold valuable information and insight that people without your experiences cannot see.

Think about specific experiences you've had in your life, the challenges you've gone through, and the solutions you used in your own life to overcome your challenges. If there was a challenge in your life that you couldn't find a solution to, what kind of solution do you wish you could have found? Write your thoughts in the columns below:

LIFE EXPERIENCE #1: ....

CHALLENGES	SOLUTIONS

LIFE EXPERIENCE #2: ....

CHALLENGES	SOLUTIONS
....	....
....	....
....	....
....	....
....	....
....	....
....	....
....	....
....	....
....	....

LIFE EXPERIENCE #3: ....

CHALLENGES	SOLUTIONS
....	....
....	....
....	....
....	....
....	....
....	....
....	....
....	....
....	....
....	....

Also think about the roles you have you played in your life (e.g. mother, sister, employee, pet owner, caretaker, business owner, car owner, student, etc.). What challenges did you have in these roles, and what solutions were you looking for, or did you find or create? Write your thoughts in the columns below:

ROLE #1: ....

CHALLENGES	SOLUTIONS

ROLE #2: ....

CHALLENGES	SOLUTIONS

ROLE #3: ....

CHALLENGES	SOLUTIONS
....	....
....	....
....	....
....	....
....	....
....	....
....	....
....	....
....	....

Finally, think about your past and/or current job(s). Think back to the major problems that you and your employer had, and the solutions you helped come up with, or you wish you could have found. Write your thoughts in the columns below:

JOB #1: ....

CHALLENGES	SOLUTIONS
....	....
....	....
....	....
....	....
....	....
....	....
....	....
....	....
....	....

JOB #2: ....

CHALLENGES	SOLUTIONS

JOB #3: ....

CHALLENGES	SOLUTIONS

Each of the challenges and solutions you discussed are actually potential customer needs and the foundation to a new business idea. Circle the top business ideas.

USE THIS SPACE TO REFLECT ON THE IDEAS YOU CAME UP WITH TODAY, AND/OR LIST ANY ADDITIONAL IDEAS YOU HAVE.

CHALLENGE 08

EVALUATE:

*to judge or determine
the significance, worth,
or quality of*

EVALUATE YOUR BUSINESS IDEAS

Now that you've generated some business ideas you'll need to evaluate them and pick one. Remember, the best business ideas fill a large customer need- one where the customer will do almost anything to obtain the solution you're offering.

Additionally, since the goal of this GAME is to make at least $1,000 in 90 days, your favorite ideas should be ideas that you:

- Are passionate and excited about
- Are knowledgeable in
- Believe there's a market for (don't worry, we'll test this)
- Are confident about

SO, GO BACK THROUGH ALL OF THE IDEA GENERATION EXERCISES, REVIEW THE IDEAS YOU CAME UP WITH, PICK 4 IDEAS BASED ON THE ABOVE GUIDE LINES, AND THEN WRITE THEM IN THE BLANKS LABELED "BUSINESS IDEA" 1-4 ON THE NEXT PAGES.

NEXT YOU WILL ASK YOURSELF THE FOLLOWING QUESTIONS ABOUT EACH IDEA:

40

BUSINESS IDEA #1: ....

WHAT IS THE NEED THAT YOU ARE FILLING WITH THIS IDEA?

....

....

....

HOW LARGE IS THIS NEED? HOW MANY PEOPLE DO YOU THINK ARE
SEEKING A SOLUTION?

....

....

....

WHO IS THE TARGET PERSON THAT HAS THIS NEED?

....

....

....

DOES THIS IDEA INTEREST AND EXCITE YOU? WHY?

....

....

....

HOW WILL YOU MAKE MONEY FROM THIS IDEA?

....

....

....

DO YOU HAVE OR COULD YOU EASILY ACQUIRE THE SKILLS AND RESOURCES TO
START THIS BUSINESS?

....

....

....

BUSINESS IDEA #2: ....

WHAT IS THE NEED THAT YOU ARE FILLING WITH THIS IDEA?

....

....

....

HOW LARGE IS THIS NEED? HOW MANY PEOPLE DO YOU THINK ARE
SEEKING A SOLUTION?

....

....

....

WHO IS THE TARGET PERSON THAT HAS THIS NEED?

....

....

....

DOES THIS IDEA INTEREST AND EXCITE YOU? WHY?

....

....

....

HOW WILL YOU MAKE MONEY FROM THIS IDEA?

....

....

....

DO YOU HAVE OR COULD YOU EASILY ACQUIRE THE SKILLS AND RESOURCES TO
START THIS BUSINESS?

....

....

....

BUSINESS IDEA #3: ....

WHAT IS THE NEED THAT YOU ARE FILLING WITH THIS IDEA?

....

....

....

HOW LARGE IS THIS NEED? HOW MANY PEOPLE DO YOU THINK ARE
SEEKING A SOLUTION?

....

....

....

WHO IS THE TARGET PERSON THAT HAS THIS NEED?

....

....

....

DOES THIS IDEA INTEREST AND EXCITE YOU? WHY?

....

....

....

HOW WILL YOU MAKE MONEY FROM THIS IDEA?

....

....

....

DO YOU HAVE OR COULD YOU EASILY ACQUIRE THE SKILLS AND RESOURCES TO
START THIS BUSINESS?

....

....

....

BUSINESS IDEA #4 ....

WHAT IS THE NEED THAT YOU ARE FILLING WITH THIS IDEA?

....

....

....

HOW LARGE IS THIS NEED? HOW MANY PEOPLE DO YOU THINK ARE
SEEKING A SOLUTION?

....

....

....

WHO IS THE TARGET PERSON THAT HAS THIS NEED?

....

....

....

DOES THIS IDEA INTEREST AND EXCITE YOU? WHY?

....

....

....

HOW WILL YOU MAKE MONEY FROM THIS IDEA?

....

....

....

DO YOU HAVE OR COULD YOU EASILY ACQUIRE THE SKILLS AND RESOURCES TO
START THIS BUSINESS?

....

....

....

ADDITIONAL THOUGHTS:

MAKE A DECISION

If you haven't already, use today to determine your favorite business idea. In order to make money with the Stress-Free Start-Up, I recommend that you pick something that would be easy to start and that you are passionate about. If you pick a complicated idea, something that requires a lot of resources, or something you are not skilled or passionate in you will be less likely to monetize the idea quickly.

If you have a dream of starting something bigger, do not give up. Understand that this game is designed to help you walk before you run, and give you a tool you can use to build the confidence, skills, and resources you will need to start and/or grow something larger.

Remember, you can change your idea at a later time, in fact, I would even suggest that you change your idea before you spend any money if one of the following happens:

- You realize there's not a large enough market for your business.
- You realize you're not passionate about the business (but be careful not to confuse fear for a lack of passion).
- You realize you do not CURRENTLY have access to the resources you need to start this business.

SO, WHAT IS YOUR FAVORITE BUSINESS IDEA?

....

....

....

RACHEL SAYS:

"If you cannot pick an idea, or you aren't happy with any of them, post a comment in the Facebook group and tell me what you're having trouble with."

CHALLENGE 10

QUICK MARKET RESEARCH

MARKET
RESEARCH:

The process of assessing whether a business ideas has a reasonable chance of success.

CONGRATULATIONS! YOU SHOULD HAVE AN IDEA TODAY. HOW DO YOU FEEL?

....

....

....

Today is about exploring your idea. First, do some research and find at least 3 other businesses that are similar to the one you plan on starting. Use the section below to brainstorm businesses that are similar to yours, then pick three specific ones and fill out the information about these "competitors" on the following pages.

BUSINESS NAME: ....

WEBSITE: ....

WHAT I LIKE ABOUT THIS COMPANY:

....

....

....

....

WHAT I WOULD DO DIFFERENTLY:

....

....

....

....

OTHER NOTES:

BUSINESS NAME: ....

WEBSITE: ....

WHAT I LIKE ABOUT THIS COMPANY:

....

....

....

....

WHAT I WOULD DO DIFFERENTLY:

....

....

....

....

OTHER NOTES:

BUSINESS NAME: ....

WEBSITE: ....

WHAT I LIKE ABOUT THIS COMPANY:

....

....

....

....

WHAT I WOULD DO DIFFERENTLY:

....

....

....

....

OTHER NOTES:

Next, you need to figure out what your customer wants, and "what you don't know you don't know" …
First, take an educated guess at who you think your target market is.

(Everyone is not an acceptable answer) …

WHAT DO YOU THINK YOUR TARGET MARKET LOOKS LIKE? (BE SPECIFIC)

....

....

....

WHAT DO YOU THINK THEY DO ON A REGULAR BASIS AND SPEND MONEY ON?
(BE SPECIFIC)

....

....

....

....

....

....

Next, define the questions you would like to ask your target market in relation to your idea. You should try to think of questions that will help you create a better product or service for them.

A sample script with questions may include (but is not limited to):

Thank you for agreeing to speak with me today. As I mentioned on the phone/in my email, I'm studying people's interest in .... (your business idea), and I welcome your views.

First, can we touch on a few biographical questions for my records?

- *What is the correct spelling of your name?*
- *In what city or town do you live?*
- *Observe, don't ask: Approximate age: .... Gender: ....*
- *Thank you, ok, first I would like to ask you if you have ever or would ever be interested in a product or service that .... (result you provide)?*
- *Why or why not?*
- *How much would you pay for a product or service that provided (what you provide)?*
- *Why?*

BRAINSTORM THE ADDITIONAL QUESTIONS YOU THINK WOULD BE USEFUL TO ASK YOUR TARGET MARKET BELOW:

....

....

....

....

....

....

....

....

....

....

....

....

....

....

A GOAL WITHOUT A PLAN IS JUST A WISH

Since you're participating in this game, I'm assuming one of your big goals is to start or grow your business. Now that you have a firm business idea, you need to determine a specific goal, and then work on developing a specific action plan to help you reach that goal. We also need to assess what your gaps are and where you will need help.

Take a moment to reflect on where you currently are, and where you would like to be in relation to your business.

WHERE I CURRENTLY AM:

....

....

....

WHERE I WOULD LIKE TO BE BY ....

....

....

....

Now, ask yourself,

"What do I need in order to successfully reach my goal?" There is no wrong answer to this, simply brainstorm what you feel and think you need to start your business.

See the example and follow the steps for effectively brainstorming your plan on the following page, and take note of the following:

- You don't need everything you think you need to start a business. To be a legitimate business you do need a business license, but I don't recommend people get that until they have made at least their first $1,000. I feel the same way about websites and logos! The main focus when you're first starting a business is to see if people really want your product or service and make some money BEFORE you start spending a lot of money on things you think you need for your business. There are always exceptions to this rule, but if you're doing this game for a business that has a lot of risk (like a construction company or medical office), this game probably isn't the best fit for you.

STEP 1: WRITE OUT YOUR ONE BIG GOAL IN THE CENTER OF THE PAGE.

BIG GOAL: Make $1,000

STEP 2: WRITE ALL THE ACCOMPLISHMENTS YOU NEED TO ACHIEVE IN ORDER TO REACH YOUR ONE BIG GOAL *(THIS IS A SIMPLIFIED VERSION FOR EXAMPLE PURPOSES ONLY).*

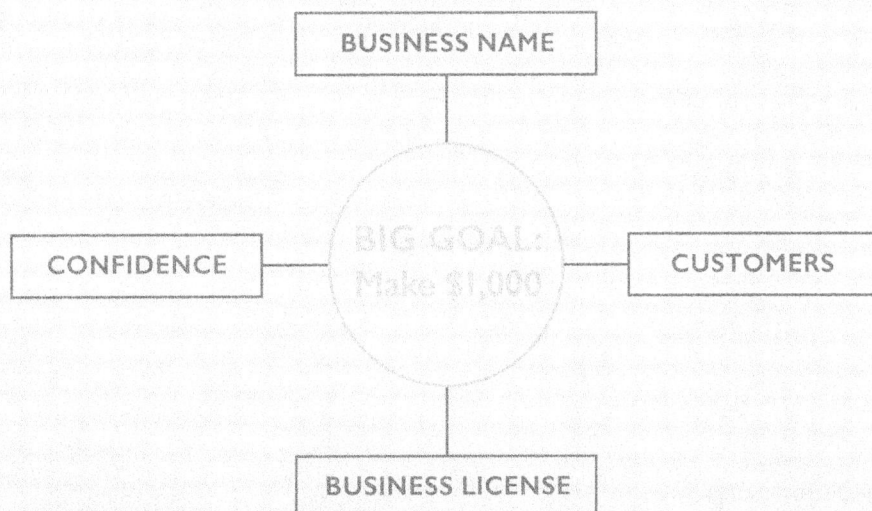

BUSINESS NAME

CONFIDENCE — BIG GOAL: Make $1,000 — **CUSTOMERS**

BUSINESS LICENSE

STEP 3: WRITE OUT ALL OF THE STEPS THAT YOU NEED TO COMPLETE TO OBTAIN EACH ACCOMPLISHMENT FROM STEP TWO. CONTINUE TO WRITE STEPS AND SUB-STEPS UNTIL YOU HAVE A SIMPLE AND CLEAR STARTING POINT TO REACHING YOUR ACCOMPLISHMENT, AND THUS, YOUR GOAL.

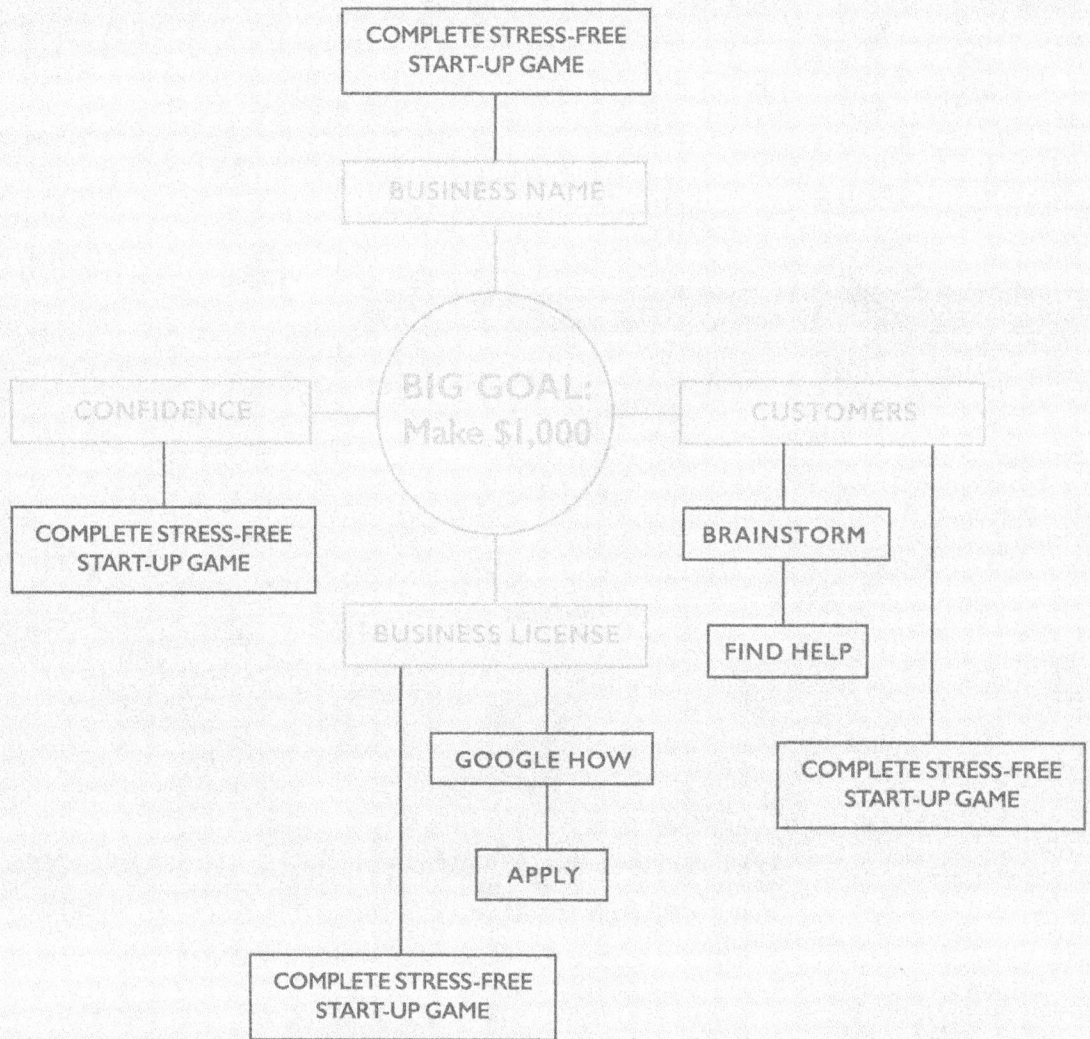

```
                    ┌──────────────────────┐
                    │ COMPLETE STRESS-FREE  │
                    │    START-UP GAME      │
                    └──────────┬───────────┘
                               │
                    ┌──────────┴───────────┐
                    │    BUSINESS NAME      │
                    └──────────┬───────────┘
                               │
                          ╭────┴────╮
  ┌─────────────┐         │ BIG GOAL:│        ┌─────────────┐
  │ CONFIDENCE  ├─────────┤ Make $1,000├──────┤  CUSTOMERS  │
  └──────┬──────┘         ╰────┬────╯         └──────┬──────┘
         │                     │                     │
┌────────┴─────────┐           │            ┌────────┴────────┐
│ COMPLETE STRESS- │           │            │   BRAINSTORM    │
│ FREE START-UP    │           │            └────────┬────────┘
│ GAME             │   ┌───────┴────────┐            │
└──────────────────┘   │ BUSINESS LICENSE│   ┌────────┴────────┐
                       └───────┬────────┘   │   FIND HELP     │
                               │            └─────────────────┘
                       ┌───────┴────────┐   ┌──────────────────┐
                       │  GOOGLE HOW    │   │ COMPLETE STRESS- │
                       └───────┬────────┘   │ FREE START-UP    │
                               │            │ GAME             │
                       ┌───────┴────────┐   └──────────────────┘
                       │     APPLY      │
                       └────────────────┘
              ┌──────────────────┐
              │ COMPLETE STRESS- │
              │ FREE START-UP    │
              │ GAME             │
              └──────────────────┘
```

56

STEP 4: LIST OUT ANYBODY INVOLVED IN ANY OF THE STEPS YOU WROTE DOWN IN STEP THREE. INCLUDE THEM EVEN IF YOU SIMPLY NEED TO ASK THEM FOR ADVICE.

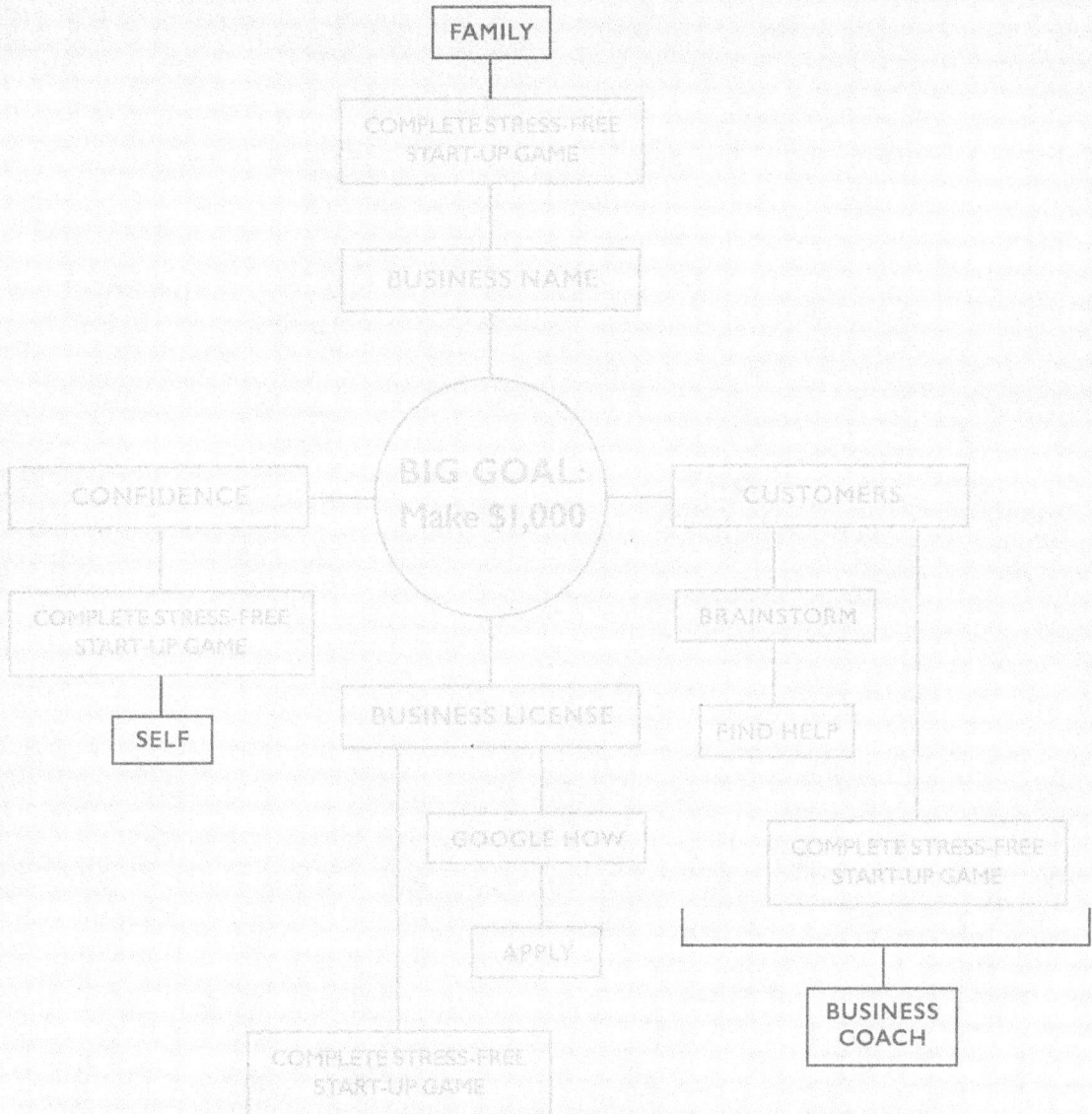

```
                        ┌──────────┐
                        │  FAMILY  │
                        └────┬─────┘
                   ┌─────────┴──────────┐
                   │ COMPLETE STRESS-FREE │
                   │   START-UP GAME     │
                   └─────────┬──────────┘
                   ┌─────────┴──────────┐
                   │   BUSINESS NAME    │
                   └─────────┬──────────┘

 ┌────────────┐         ╱          ╲         ┌────────────┐
 │ CONFIDENCE │──────( BIG GOAL:   )──────│  CUSTOMERS │
 └─────┬──────┘       ( Make $1,000 )      └─────┬──────┘
 ┌─────┴────────────┐    ╲        ╱         ┌────┴───────┐
 │ COMPLETE STRESS- │                       │ BRAINSTORM │
 │ FREE START-UP    │                       └────┬───────┘
 │ GAME             │      │                ┌────┴───────┐
 └─────┬────────────┘      │                │ FIND HELP  │
 ┌─────┴──────┐     ┌──────┴────────┐       └────┬───────┘
 │   SELF     │     │ BUSINESS LICENSE│      ┌────┴──────────────┐
 └────────────┘     └──────┬────────┘       │ COMPLETE STRESS-FREE│
                    ┌──────┴────────┐        │   START-UP GAME    │
                    │  GOOGLE HOW   │        └────────┬───────────┘
                    └──────┬────────┘                 │
                    ┌──────┴────────┐          ┌──────┴──────┐
                    │    APPLY      │          │  BUSINESS   │
                    └──────┬────────┘          │   COACH     │
          ┌───────────────┴──────┐            └─────────────┘
          │ COMPLETE STRESS-FREE  │
          │   START-UP GAME       │
          └───────────────────────┘
```

STEP 5: LIST OUT ANY REWARDS YOU WOULD LIKE TO GIVE YOURSELF FOR ACHIEVING ANY OF STEPS OR ACCOMPLISHMENTS THAT YOU HAVE LISTED. YOU DO NOT HAVE TO HAVE A REWARD FOR EVERY STEP OR ACCOMPLISHMENT, BUT YOU CAN IF YOU WOULD LIKE TO, ESPECIALLY IF THERE IS A CERTAIN STEP OR ACCOMPLISHMENT THAT YOU FIND YOURSELF BEING AFRAID TO ACHIEVE.

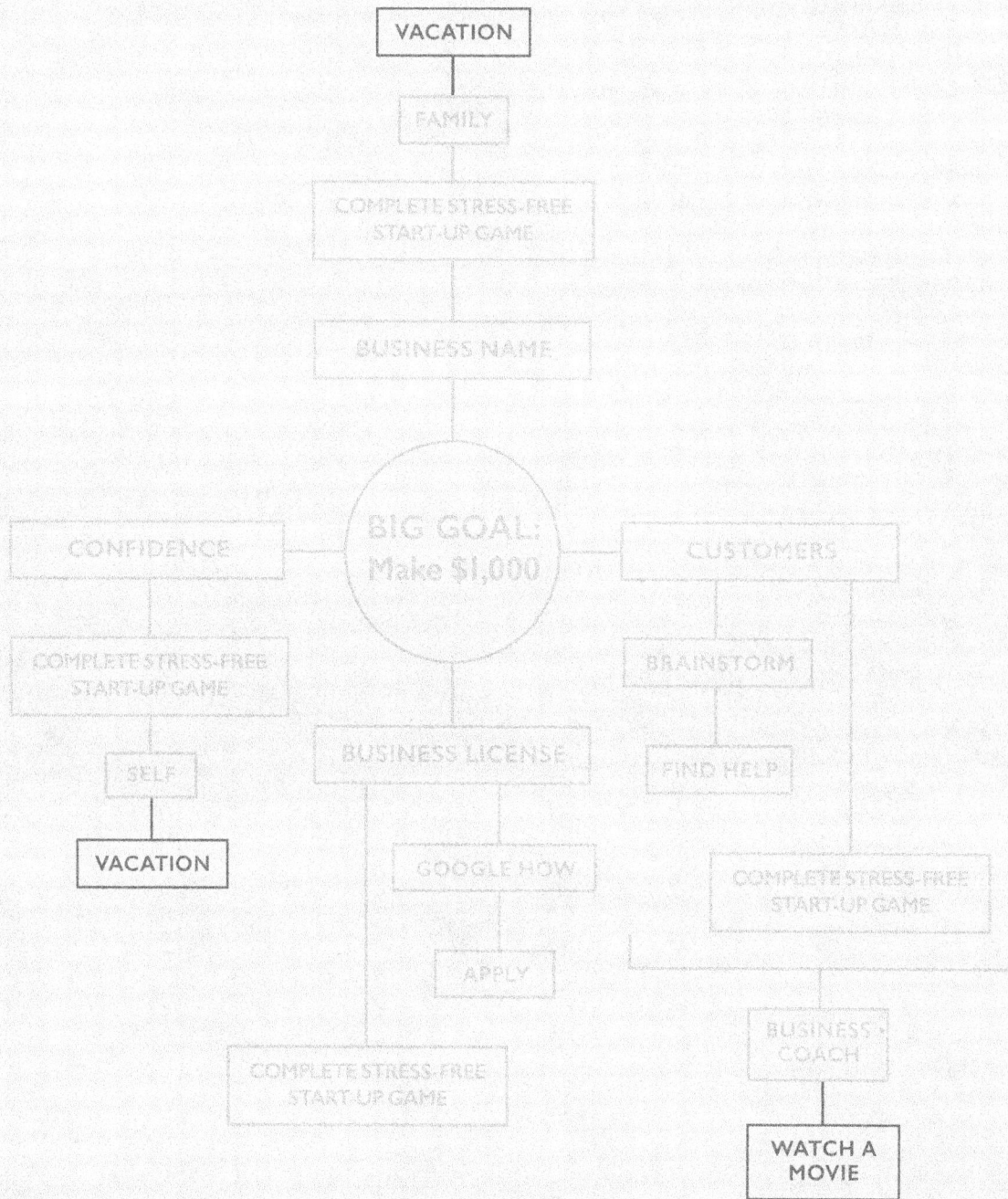

VACATION

FAMILY

COMPLETE STRESS-FREE START-UP GAME

BUSINESS NAME

BIG GOAL: Make $1,000

CONFIDENCE

CUSTOMERS

COMPLETE STRESS-FREE START-UP GAME

BRAINSTORM

SELF

BUSINESS LICENSE

FIND HELP

VACATION

GOOGLE HOW

COMPLETE STRESS-FREE START-UP GAME

APPLY

BUSINESS COACH

COMPLETE STRESS-FREE START-UP GAME

WATCH A MOVIE

STEP 6: PRIORITIZE THE ORDER IN WHICH YOU NEED TO COMPLETE THE
STEPS AND ACCOMPLISHMENTS YOU WROTE DOWN.

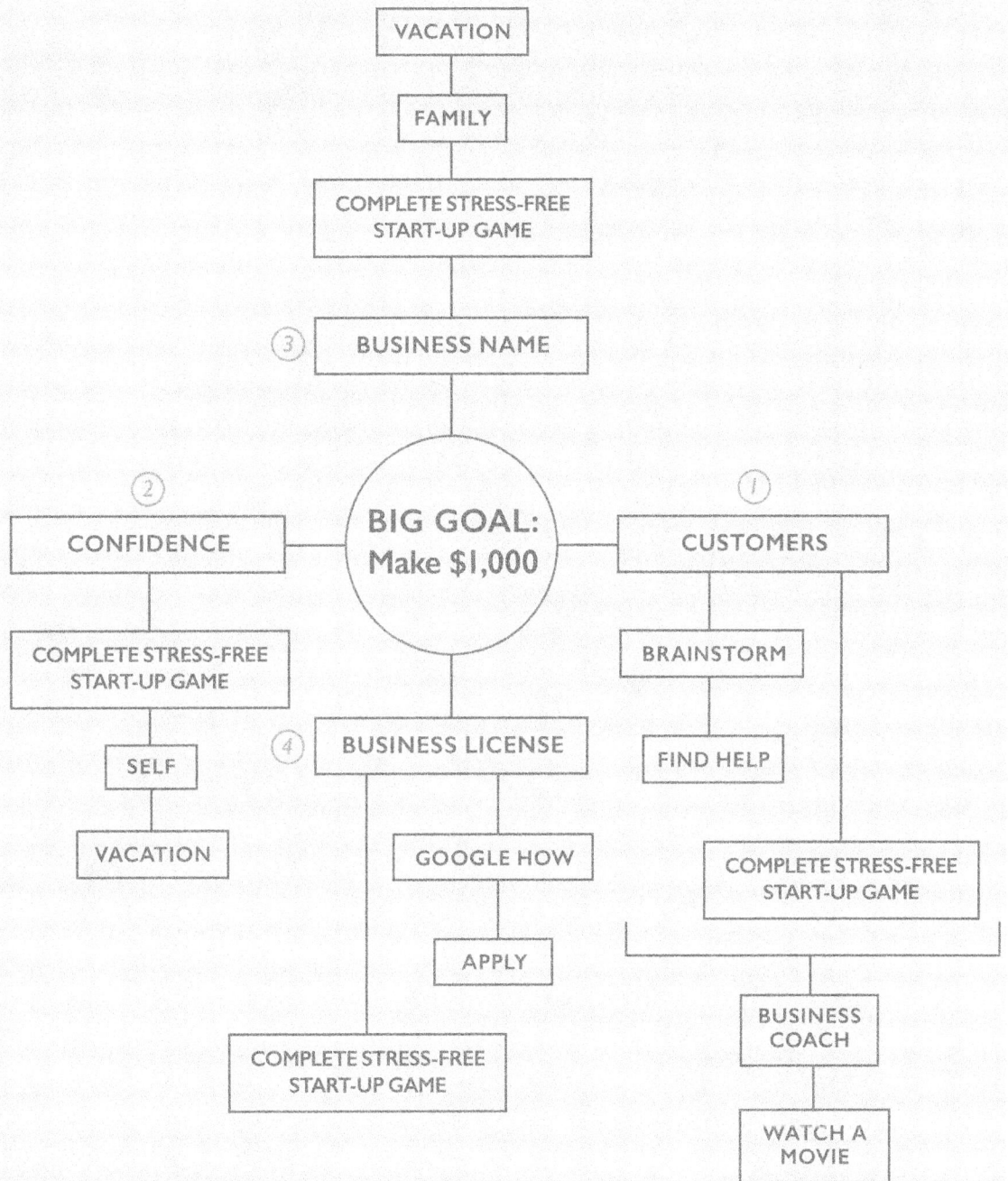

VACATION

FAMILY

COMPLETE STRESS-FREE
START-UP GAME

③ BUSINESS NAME

② CONFIDENCE — BIG GOAL: Make $1,000 — CUSTOMERS ①

COMPLETE STRESS-FREE
START-UP GAME

SELF

VACATION

④ BUSINESS LICENSE

BRAINSTORM

FIND HELP

GOOGLE HOW

APPLY

COMPLETE STRESS-FREE
START-UP GAME

COMPLETE STRESS-FREE
START-UP GAME

BUSINESS
COACH

WATCH A
MOVIE

CHALLENGE 12

SUPPORT TEAM:

A person or group of people (paid or unpaid) that agree to provide comfort, assistance, and/ or encouragement to you.

BUILD YOUR SUPPORT TEAM

Yesterday you thought about the people who can help you accomplish specific tasks that are related to the business that you want to start or grow. Today, think about who else your support team will be in starting this business. Who will be your trusted advisors, mentors, and accountability partners that you will lean on when you need support?

More importantly, especially in the start-up phase of a business, who will pick up the things that you drop. For example, if you are usually responsible for doing all the housework, who can you lean on to help you with this so you can have more time to invest in your business? List these people and the roles they will take below:

SUPPORT TEAM	HOW THEY WILL SUPPORT YOU

Now, ask them if they are willing to be on your team, and communicate their responsibilities (how they need to support you).

CHALLENGE 13

BRAINSTORM YOUR TARGET MARKET: PART 1

Put simply, a target market is a particular group of consumers at which a product or service is aimed. A target market is important because it allows you to focus your marketing time, money, messaging, and energy on a specific market that is more likely to buy from you than other markets.

Here's an example: If I decided to start a speed dating event in the county of Riverside, and I sent postcards to every home in the county, my marketing would be very expensive. What's worse is that I would've wasted a lot of money because I would've sent mail to people who aren't interested in dating: people who are married, in committed relationships, etc.

For you to save thousands of dollars on marketing, it's vital that you define your target market.

FUN FACT

Sometimes the business idea you have has things in common with you (or an older/younger version of yourself)! This is especially true if you have or had a pain or a frustration that you solved for yourself, and now you would like to share the solution with the world. Today we're going to explore the type of consumer you are... You may find valuable insight about your target market after assessing yourself as a consumer.

First, think about the version of yourself that would most appreciate your business idea. Is it the teenage you, the current you, an older version of yourself, or someone in between?

Next, imagine that you are currently the version of yourself that would most appreciate your business idea. Answer the following questions about the version of yourself that would most appreciate your business idea. Try to be specific and give as much detail as possible. Don't judge your answers; just write out the answer the way the version of you that you're considering would answer:

WHAT'S YOUR ETHNICITY?

....

WHAT'S YOUR GENDER?

....

HOW OLD ARE YOU?

....

WHAT GENERATION DO YOU BELONG TO (E.G. BABY BOOMERS, GEN X, ETC.)?

....

WHAT'S YOUR HOUSING SITUATION (OWN, RENT, HOME TYPE, HOME VALUE, HOME LOCATION)?

....

WHAT'S YOUR EDUCATIONAL BACKGROUND (SCHOOLS YOU WENT TO, DEGREES YOU'VE EARNED, ETC.)?

....

....

....

....

WHAT ARE YOUR POLITICAL AND RELIGIOUS VIEWS?

....

....

WHAT LANGUAGES DO YOU SPEAK?

....

....

WHAT'S YOUR FINANCIAL SITUATION?

....

....

....

....

....

....

WHAT'S YOUR EMPLOYMENT SITUATION (EMPLOYED/UNEMPLOYED/SELF-
EMPLOYED; WHAT INDUSTRY DO YOU WORK IN; WHAT'S YOUR JOB TITLE;
WHO'S YOUR EMPLOYER, ETC.)?

....

....

....

....

WHAT'S YOUR RELATIONSHIP SITUATION (LIST ALL THAT YOU CAN THINK OF, E.G.
MOTHER, SISTER, WIFE, GRANDMOTHER, SINGLE, MARRIED, ETC.)?

....

....

....

....

WHAT KIND OF LIFESTYLE DO YOU LEAD?

....

....

....

....

WHAT KIND OF EVENTS DO YOU GO TO?

....

....

....

....

WHAT'S MOST IMPORTANT TO YOU RIGHT NOW?

....

....

....

....

WHAT KEEPS YOU UP AT NIGHT?

....

....

....

....

WHAT DO YOU DO FOR FUN?

....

....

....

....

WHAT ARE YOUR HOBBIES?

....

....

....

....

WHERE DO YOU SPEND YOUR TIME (BE SPECIFIC, TRY WALKING THROUGH YOUR AVERAGE WEEK... WHERE DO YOU GO?)

....

....

....

....

WHAT DO YOU READ OFFLINE?

....

....

....

....

WHAT DO YOU READ ONLINE (BE SPECIFIC)?

....

....

....

....

WHAT SOCIAL MEDIA SITES (IF ANY) DO YOU USE? CIRCLE THE ONES YOU USE THE MOST.

....

....

....

....

WHAT DO YOU WATCH?

. . . .

. . . .

. . . .

. . . .

WHAT DO YOU LISTEN TO?

. . . .

. . . .

. . . .

. . . .

WHAT STORES DO YOU FREQUENT?

. . . .

. . . .

. . . .

. . . .

WHAT MAJOR LIFE EVENT ARE YOU EXPERIENCING OR PREPARING FOR? (E.G.
NEW RELATIONSHIP, WEDDING, PREGNANCY, RETIREMENT, COLLEGE, MOVING,
TRAVELING, JOB CHANGE, ETC.)

. . . .

. . . .

. . . .

. . . .

CHALLENGE 14

REAL MARKET RESEARCH

Starting today, you need to speak to people both inside and outside of your network about your business idea.

Your goal is to successfully talk to and get answers from a minimum of 10 people about your business idea - 5 of those people need to be people you've never met.

Over the next few days you need to go to the location (online or offline) where you think your target market is hanging out (see yesterday's exercise), approach the people you think would be your target market, tell them what you are working on, that you value their opinion and ideas, and ask them if they would be willing to speak with you so you can run some ideas by them (you may want to bribe them with a small reward for their time).

Ask them the questions you developed from Challenge 10. Also, try to think of the things you know you don't know that you want to know about your target market. Take notes. You may even want to audio record the meeting so you can listen to what they said later.

Make sure you go somewhere in public, and make sure you are safe. It may help if you have someone comes with you.

Remember, you can make $1,000 or more with this game, but you have to take action and do the challenges.

If you're feeling anxious, nervous or scared, feel free to ask for help from me, and/or from the other people in the game. You may even want to ask the other people from the game to go with you if you have similar target markets.

Need motivation? Go watch the Art Williams Just Do It Speech on YouTube.

To be held accountable, find a mentor and share the following information with them or post an update on the Facebook group of what you've done for today. Make sure you include:

- How many people you tried to contact today
- The way you tried to contact people today
- How many people you successfully communicated with today
- A recap of any interviews you've conducted today

RECAP

Over the past 14 days you should have successfully:

- Assessed your talents, gifts and strengths
- Destroyed your limiting beliefs
- Determined what motivates you
- Chosen specific life goals
- Learned how to stop making excuses
- Come up with tons of new ideas
- Strategically evaluated your ideas
- Made a decision
- Researched your competitors
- Outlined a strategic plan
- Built your support team
- Figured out your target market
- Done market research

How does it feel?

You can pat yourself on the back because by completing these exercises you've done things that most business owners never do, and believe me, they pay for it later.

So, what's next?

By going through the exercises in this workbook you may have realized your business idea needs some work. If that's the case, simply use the knowledge you've gained to make adjustments to your business idea.

If you realized there wasn't a market for the business you want to start, simply revisit a different idea you came up with and do market research for that idea. Another option is to start from the beginning and come up with more ideas.

If you couldn't get through these exercises, ask yourself if you're really ready to be an entrepreneur right now. Believe me, being an entrepreneur takes consistent work every single day when you're first getting started. If you couldn't bother to do these exercises, what will drive you when it comes to working on your business? I'm not here to discourage you, but rather to suggest an area for improvement before you commit your hard earned money to something you're not quite ready for.

Finally, if you successfully got through these exercises, got positive market feedback when you were doing research, and feel excited about your business idea, you're ready for the next step. I have 76 more challenges for people committed to their success. To get the next week of challenges for free simply go to www.TheStressFreeStartup.com/week3.

You have reached the end of the Stress-Free Start-Up. Interested in continuing your business journey with more challenges?

Get the next week of challenges for free by going to www.TheStressFreeStartup.com/week3 and for additional resources on starting a business go to www.TalkRaw.org

 /TalkRaw   @TalkRaw   @TalkRaw_   TalkRaw